ABOUT THE AUTHOR

Evrah Rose is known for her fearless energy and hard-hitting poetry. Not one to shy away from a tough subject - Evrah has produced a number of thought-provoking viral videos, racking up over 5 million video hits on social media. Her first musical release, *Labyrinth* (2017), was aired by Adam Walton via BBC Introducing on BBC Radio Wales within the first few days of its release. Evrah has since been a regular feature on BBC Radio Wales and radio stations across North East Wales and the Midlands. Evrah released her debut poetry collection - *Unspoken* (VERVE Poetry Press, September 2019) launching in both Waterstones, Birmingham and Bank St. Social in her beloved hometown of Wrexham.

Evrah has featured on many BBC and ITV social media and TV platforms, including live radio features from Adam Walton, Huw Stephens and Janice Long, BBC Radio Wales. Along with commissions for; BBC Sport Wales, Shelter Cymru, Homestart and BBC Two. In September 2022 Evrah was the opener for Chwarae Tegs Womenspire Awards on ITV Wales. Evrah has become a prominent voice in Wales, in both poetry and football circles, and amongst those dedicated to social causes.

Evrah has enjoyed residencies at both Ty Pawb, and Wrexham AFC and worked with a number of organisations and educational facilities including, local primary and secondary schools, Colleges, Glyndŵr University, Expo Wal Goch and HMP Berwyn, providing workshops to students and young people to promote a positive sense of self and mental health wellbeing, using writing as an outlet of expression. As part of the BBC's centenary UK tour 2022, Evrah was selected as a BBC Bitesize panel member, visiting secondary schools in Wales to discuss careers in storytelling.

As someone who's suffered extensively with her health Evrah is working with health and social care professionals and creatives to develop holistic well-being services that empower individuals. Encouraging and supporting them via engaging, educational and transparent programs to reduce patient passivity, and increase control over their own health and mental well-being. Tackling the hierarchical barriers currently in place that often leave patients feeling disempowered.

Evrah has performed and headlined events throughout the UK; from Spoken Trend, Birmingham, The Homeless World Cup and Hub Festival, Cardiff to the Racecourse Football Stadium before a crowd of 7000 Wrexham AFC fans. Along the way, supporting well-known artists from Sabrina Benaim (Button Poetry) to Beans on Toast. Evrah has become a strong voice in the movement to end violence against women. Working alongside Gŵyl y Ferch, Evrahs poetry film 'Will You Be Coming Back?' was exhibited at Oriel Mon, Llangefni to raise awareness of domestic violence occurring in same-sex relationships. In November 2022, Evrah featured in Welsh Womens Aid, 'Live Fear Free' film campaign supported by White Ribbon UK and the FAW to highlight and take a stand against gender-based violence.

'Evrah Rose is a voice that speaks for working class Wales and those who are on the margins. She is fearless, noisy, tenacious, radical and real. Seren go iawn.' **Leanne Wood**

Evrah Rose
Define Hope

VERVE
POETRY PRESS
BIRMINGHAM

PUBLISHED BY VERVE POETRY PRESS
https://vervepoetrypress.com
mail@vervepoetrypress.com

All rights reserved
© 2023 Evrah Rose

The right of Evrah Rose to be identified as author of this work has been asserted in accordance with section 77 of the Copyright, Designs and Patents Act 1988.

No part of this work may be reproduced, stored or transmitted in any form or by any means, graphic, electronic, recorded or mechanical, without the prior written permission of the publisher.

FIRST PUBLISHED MAY 2023

Printed and bound in the UK
by ImprintDigital, Exeter

ISBN: 978-1-913917-37-1

Cover and interior illustrations by Ellie Humphreys

'You have weak bones'

CONTENTS

What Do You Know?	11
Little Brown Book	12
Click	16
Don't Forget to Remember Me	20
American Dreams	22
The Elephant and The Trampoline	24
Pride and Prejudice	28
Daddy's Little Girl	33
You Will Always Be	37
The City Part II	39
Ashes in the Snow	43
All You Ever Say	46
Evrah Introduces Jo Marsh	50
After Nepotism Gains Everyone Loses	53
Run Away	58
Let Them Eat Cake	61
Lol. Why are you crying?	64
My Sister's Keeper	69
Sign Anguish	73
Twelve Thirty-Three	75
Imprints	77
Call Me Home	78
Role Models	82

Cycles	85
All I Need Is Time	88
Wander Gently as You Go	90
For Every Step	92
I left you once	94
D E F I N E H O P E	96

Acknowledgements

Define Hope

For Aria
Fly on, Cariad.

What Do You Know?

La, do you remember the Wrexham Lager scent,
that wandered with us down our street?
Towards that tiny house with the creepy false teeth?
Its overgrowth and broken windows were always beautiful to me.
And the stones that tripped our Reebok covered feet,
we'd throw
carefree
across the same train tracks I'd eventually use to leave
the love, the town that - raised me.
What do they know about me?

Am I humble or arrogant?
Dismissive or forgiving?
What do you know about me?

Am I stubborn or tenacious?
Reckless or gracious?
Tell me all you know about me.

Am I weak or dangerous?
Cowardly or courageous?
What is it you *think* you know about me?

Because, I come from "nothing", they say.
Hailed from a world without silver spoons.
Diamonds or pearls just...
Humble beginnings.
What do you know about me.

What do you *really*
know about me?

Little Brown Book

I know what's coming now, her intent, that sour look.
I can feel the air change and begin to crowd my lungs.
I'm nervous wondering what type of hate will rouse – cause'.
She's about to go get out her little brown book.

She loves to patronise, calculate, and round up.
Kill my financial freedom and ability from the - ground up.
Trapped in hardship those footsteps are the awful sounds of,
her searching, reaching for her little brown book.

I ask her why we never look at hers.
Why it's always -

My bank.
My money.
My phone.

She claims I'm controlling her. I'm sneaky.
Quizzes on what I'm hiding, really?
Yet, I don't get privacy.
Every letter that arrives for me she - mithers me.
Who's that from?
Let me open it!
Why are you denying me?
My mum and dad open each other's mail.
It's all right for them. It's fine with me.

Every bill is in my name.
All of the financial responsibility.
It's my pain.
I've been taking out credit just to maintain
myself.

I can't pay the 'Pay Day' loans,
or credit cards,
the debts are racking up.
Now they're writing and calling me,
several times each day.
Every penny of mine is claimed,
Shame and anxiety
I start to shake at the till.
Will my card decline?
The worry has me ill.
Monzo empty pots,
direct debits bouncing
naughts.
Fraught,
never knowing how I'll pay the lot.
Nightmares of bailiffs knocking doors and
changing locks.
She needs to know who's paying me
when and what.
Pushes constantly to know what my balance is
and what I've got.
She lacks transparency,
yet, I'm the one accused of dishonesty.
It's a haphazardly environment in which I'm lost.

She prefers to have me work less,
It keeps me reliant.
Silent and compliant.
Denies she's anything, nothing, no surplus.
Claims she's brassy to her parents.
All of this has its purpose.
Every move is pre-planned - plotted.
I'm berated whilst out shopping
for simply wanting a Flake.
Onlookers glance awkwardly,
as she lightens up her face.

A friendly smile followed with;
'Pick it up, yes – okay'.
She loves to state with malice
how she loathes buying food.
The cost is such a waste.
I'm eating less daily,
more losses to my weight.
Gaunt faced and ribs displayed.
Swift kicks, precision hate.
Had me crying and screaming on
Christmas day.

She switches frequently from outrage to tame,
kindness kindled for the stage.
I find her hard to gauge.
Tip toe walking around the place.
For now,
I must play this game.
Survival is the only aim.
I must continue to reside modestly within this cage.
Keep my mouth shut,
be good, be brave – behave.
A little peace now and then must be worth these chains?
Whilst quietly, defiantly crafting
plans of my escape.

She's back again, with a brew and pen.
Taking joy in halving tens.
Alluding spends for me are a luxury,
and then removing them.
After all,
I'm useless with this poor mobility,
and speech impediment.
Why the hell would I need cash cards?
I won't be using them.

Open up your banking app,
come on - let's count some sums.
What's this extra money here then?
Sixty pounds, huh?
I've been hiding pennies; she knows
now her pen is out – fuck.
She's wanting figures and digits for her little brown book.

I fight back.
She denies all of her lies - but,
I'm the one accused forever and always on trial - looked,
at the payslips, she has my savings
as her money just - piles up.
All the while I'm scrimping,
written into her
fucking
vile
book.

Click

I look around and see how our shared commonalities have degraded.
How – so much time has been wasted.
The things we could have said, didn't say or, simply wouldn't.
The balance of respect and authentic thought,
replaced with – baseless accusations.
Apparently, 'every day is a gift'.
Is that a bribe or a statement?
It feels cursive.
Strait-laced lips parting with illusionary intention.
'The world needs saving. I'm going to save it'.
Claim you aim to diminish this widespread hatred.
Hashtag like you're genuinely advocating,
that blatant faecal scented fragrance.
It looks awfully like the hatred you spit,
if another disagrees with your blind,
fact-less,
over opinionated abrasives.

Mate, you nailed it!

We fill our plates with – more anger.
More shameless, hastily created conspiracy.

'Only Sheeple refuse to follow the misinformation you're generating'.
Wait, if...?

We need, no. We cling to – saviours.
Fictional characters created by overpriced big production,
flicks and "reality" tv - extrapolating the self-esteem issues,
we spend our days hiding.
Embodying the fallacy we're so focussed on maintaining.

I'm an all knowing – all seeing – all currency,
knowledge owning - history making,
shape shifting - grave shift hating,
imposter syndromed - smile faking,
soul breaking - empathy dissipating,
scam generating,
influencer.

*'The media are manipulating us– don't listen,
do your own research'. 'Google isn't a valid source of information'.*

Please, like my pic,
swipe – scroll – click.
Ah, I feel validated.
Omg, I love your manufactured self.
Look at the masterpiece you've created.
I'm sure the virtual public really do appreciate it.
The gaping spaces created via our own fictions.
Instagram filters for those,
"Goals we're out there chasing".
The head-shots and toxically positive quotes are truly convincing.
And we say it all without even flinching.
Poker face. King Pin.
Mirrored specs,
fresh haircuts – trim, trimmed.
Healthy eating and perfectly poached eggs.
I'm in the gym, gym
(not crying in the kitchen).
Six am starts. I'm so productive – win, wins!
Luxurious clean sheets without a crease in,
won't photograph the bed you haven't been in.
(Anxiety induced palpitations never stop you from sleeping).

Sat slouched on the couch,
refreshing the feed – every min, mins.
Needing strangers to validate

and love your – skin, skinned.
No plans for eating today?
You're summer ready – slim, slimmed.
Carvery and laughter with "friends",
uneaten pizza in the bin, binned.
Public displays of charity,
I live to – give, gives.
I'm not financially broke,
not struggling to – live, lives.
Numerous empty bottles,
just one more – gin, ginned.
Maybe it will stop you from sinking again?
Grim, grimmed.
Ambient lighting for those pixel-perfect – grin, grins.
How we glisten within this
social media paradox.
An illusion of such – skilled, skill.
What progress and vision.
It doesn't hurt one bit,
it doesn't – kill, kills.
I'm doing fine. I'm not fractured,
not – ill, illed.

I'm an icon – brand wearing,
inspiration sharing - cocktail sipping,
never slipping - mental health not dipping,
never jaw clenching – frustrated, hair ripping.

Much adoration for those savvy features
fixing our facial splitting,
designed to smoothen out those cracks,
the realism and emotional spillage.
Let's pillage each other's fakery,
become nothing like we'd all envisaged.
Who cares if we no longer reflect our own mirrors image?

At least we're distracted,
from the pain that is daily living.

Wake up and you dress. Make up for the stress.
Hide your pain and distress. Look at you - you're a mess.
The faking never ends. Too ashamed to confess,
you're waiting for your death.
Clearly, you're depressed.

Heaving every step.
Aching haven't slept.
Shaking from the meds. Maintain another breath.
Every day, don't forget, It brings you close to the end.
Maybe soon you can rest?

Rest in peace.

Don't Forget to Remember Me

If I hear them call to me, from across the realms of time.
If whoever makes the choice, should claim me back tonight.
And all who I love, were to hold out their hands and cry,
as I take my last breath,
right before their very eyes.
Would you focus on my wrongs?
Or come to realise,
deep within my heart I felt that all I did was right?
Will these words of mine live on?
Would you care to share the lines?
I'd carefully constructed with detailed pictures of a life;
coated in many shades,
the slopes and countless nights,
I'd broken only to re-repair, collect myself and fight.

Will my story bounce and echo
as my presence departs your sides?
Or become an unlabelled fable to slowly alter and die?
Will my honesty be praised?
Will my truths be scrutinised?
Would there be a lasting respect for all I had to say?
Would death strip me of my pride?

Something that which I,
fought so hard to keep.
Will my ending be dignified,
upon my final sleep?
And like many before me
will I simply disappear?
Will I fade into the ground
as a distant memory?

Will I lie alone, within an empty grave?
Would anyone even miss me?
Would they visit every day?
When Autumn dulls our skies,
would those leaves be swept away?
Or left for many seasons,
eventually decades?
Will I be thought of often?
Or forgotten and replaced?
Just as quickly as I died,
along with every mental moment made?
With all of my achievements,
and everything I'd tried to change?
Am I deserving of a eulogy?
Will I be just another gravelled grave?

Will I live on in your words,
As does history on each page?
Will my humble legacy,
stand the tests of time and age?
Would it be worthy of reflection,
as anything considered great?
Will my premature ending,
be another fall from grace?
Just a brief novelty,
a useless passing phase?
And, like all phases,
will my life become a waste?

All I ask of this world is
I am at least remembered.
That all I had become,
will be in some way,
loved
and treasured.

American Dreams

When I wrote Ring o' Roses, no one cared to notice.
Despite its importance it was considered, outspoken.
And some years on, suddenly there's focus.
People are outraged, rightfully so - it's,
day after day,
more children and teachers murdered.
More families destroyed,
more communities
broken.
More fear erupts. Many more become hopeless.
More screams, more trauma,
more hands to shoulders.
More loss, more grief,
further speculative motives.
More 'thoughts and prayers',
vague obituary motifs.
Pro-life painted on the walls by the same hands who vote guns in.

How many bullets does it take to steal a breath?
How many more saved if they'd repeal, enact, amend?
The second amendment is more important
than the lives of those
who wish to grow, smile and love.
Who wake daily with the fear of one day,
never waking up.

This dream you quote, do you really believe it?
These freedoms you chant, are they worth children screaming?
Is it brave to shelter under classroom desks?
Is a home so wholesome when there is no one left?

Dystopian Realities. Everyday A Mass Slaughter.
Democrat? Republican? Everyday A Mass Slaughter.
Democracy? Repression. Every Day A Mass Slaughter.
Destitute. Rich. Everyday A Mass Slaughter.
Derail. Retaliate. Everyday A Mass Slaughter.
Destroy. Reciprocate. Everyday A Mass Slaughter.
Disregard Responsibility. Everyday A Mass Slaughter.

Deadly
Repercussions
Everyday
A
Mass
Slaughter.

The Elephant and The Trampoline

Step right up to your favourite show.
The strong charms of your parading, favourite, ghost.
Who hides who she is, maintaining the goal,
of never showing people how she's near ready to blow.
She's heavy to hold though, thinner than most.
A tough, rough image to elicit control.
It's the only thing in life she feels she's able to own.
Too close to smashing up the living room, putting
kicks through the doors.

'Oh, girl - you're amazing.
So inspiring.
I don't know how you walk, how you're smiling.
That's a mountain too great yet, you climb it.
How niche, how defining'.

They romanticise the struggle but,
it's one that's undiminishing.
Clown face on, fake shoes I keep filling in.
I do another funny,
and make jokes,
I'm the Riddler.
Dithering a no,
there's a crowd to consider – it's
showtime.

I am so sick of this.
I wake daily with a bitter grin.
I'm fine this time – here's a little pic,
for Instagram, fist pump with a triple kiss - mwah.

Another coffee and a cigarette.
I act calm yet, I'm in a mess.
I laugh hard, sink to deeper depths.
My wit's dry yet, I'm dripping wet.

People never let up, with this idealising - messed up,
attitude towards ill health – look,
at the way they clap and step up.
Indulge this fucked up fetish,
for those who suffer – pleasure,
in the agony as they throw pledges,
of support that dwindle – end up,

just another idle gesture.

They're never there, they couldn't care less.
Uncomfortable should I ever question,
the fragility of their intentions.
I've no choice but, play pretension.
Now, I'm left with fake and clever,
friendships mostly fickle, fair-weather.
Can't be honest, can't be sharing,
I must glamour up this terror.

Forcing me to shut down – shell up,
is a push into the hell of,
being poorly represented.
You want positive so, I pretend that,
I'm not breaking here – not fed up.
Hide the pulling of depression.
Daren't drop the mask, they're so dependent.
They all prefer me silent – never,

speaking openly,

I seldom have the chance to crack or – well up.
Don't show emotions to them – better,
to be fictional – not bearer,
inspirational – not dwell on,
the agony - distort my present.
Now all I have is what I'm wearing.
They crave, applaud the unrelenting,
battle, fatigue, unease – the stressors.

Stage calling me it's time to dress up.
Be the face, the story telling,
fighter, advocate, shape bender.
Take your seats, I hear them yelling.
'Ladies and gentlemen,
It's Evrahhhhhhh'

s h o w t i m e.

*People only hear, only listen,
when we're gone, when we finally give in.
I'll just hide my wants of ending this,
for your benefit,
until the pain ends its grip,
and I am done living.*

Pride and Prejudice

It's June, people,
where our community becomes fashionable.
the sheer pretence.
Every summer the mirage of support,
cheer all month, where's your voice all year then?
When another loses their life, another peer again?
With the job losses, treatment denials and protests to our existence?
Where are you when a teen is disowned by their relatives?
Or January when there's no end to the tears, friend?

I'm grateful to the organisations who share their profits with our causes.
I appreciate those who walk with us and for us.

However,
when I see our rainbow,
our symbol of struggle and resistance in
corporate windows,
printed on mugs in coffee shops,
and witness onlookers allow slurs and aggression in public
it does make me wonder.
What really is there in it – for us?

I don't want to hear you talk Pride without action.
Do not invade our parades and spaces if your only goal is a cheap drink,
party and Instagram caption.
We welcome you kindly but,
I cannot stay silent when I hear such hypocritical drivel.
Where is your influence beyond this month,
beyond the – glitter visuals?
It's highly likely I will offend with this disposition.
If you're more offended by my stress of this,
than the lack of relative, progressive

and genuine attempt to end the fatal sentiments then...
I have very little time to listen.
I won't listen.
I won't cower,
or shrink into the spaces you "allow" us,
to fill with colour.

We are more than a parade,
we have pain that never ceases.
I cannot kill my persistence in my persistence, for rights and safety.
Not until my brothers and sisters of varying skin colours and religions
can walk freely and safely,
without repercussions or persecution.
Not until my trans siblings are recognised as,
Fucking human!
Until healthcare, education and employment are no longer
red taped in refusal.
When people stop arguing over our rights.
When moral issues are no longer weaponised by politicians,
who never follow through.

We see your fictional solidarity.

These businesses so laced in support
remove the flag come first of July.
Say you're supportive,
Huns, why dya' lie?
Only share our message for profit.
Merch sales, shirts with rainbow pockets.
Jest about diversity in your employment,
we're so important for your ticks in boxes.
'Where's my straight Pride'
Lol, you've already got it.
Every programme, Google map image and Disney character
has hetero, cisgender normalcy sprayed upon it.
Cards, wedding venues, music videos and advertisements -

the list is much longer than I care to bother with.
You cannot avoid it whilst you're out shopping.

So much talk of sin.
You claim it's "our choice".
We, 'ram it down your throat'.
That we should refrain, we should - stop it!
You ask five-year-old girls if they have a boyfriend.
I'd say that's forceful. What would you call it?
Your shameful, ignorant discrimination
is generally followed by talk of tradition,
wartime, conservative rhetoric.
Your symbolics murdered Alan Turing.
You may have, but we,
haven't forgotten this.

How can you define a diverse people with only a single word?
How can you articulate a vibrancy so great,
so dynamic
it colours the entire world?
Many wear us as a tokenistic badge,
yet, never defend us.
Pronouns abused, revoked, or mislabelled,
to offend us.
You can talk proudly of love and friendships without whim.
Yet, we cannot celebrate our multiple sexualities,
and non-conforming genders?

Every letter in our acronym is an extended family member.
If you're here to gain from our pain every June without intention,
only to put our colours on sale come September.
If you do not seek to break down the barriers
that suffocate and oppress us,
please, remember;
you in no way represent us with your business ventures.
Quit the pointless pretension.

And whilst you're at it,
take down our flag!
You have no right to use,
our family emblem.

'Human rights aren't political issues. They are moral issues abused by politicians.'

Daddy's Little Girl

Do you remember how we'd spar in the kitchen,
lifting weights to build my muscle and my diligence?
I was bullied big – you'd tell me this,
'Never cower, never dip and they would quit if I never did'.
You were right, I threw my punches into bigger kids.
You took me to karate class because I was needing discipline.
In need of lessons in respect,
and it leveraged my development.
When I cried about that Kata,
you killed the fears of never getting it – right,
straightened up my stance and I was fine.

I got my belts,
took the rounds and won my fights.
You taught me to never worry about my size,
'Lock eyes when you stand'.
You were proud to have a daughter with those trophies in her hands.
You had dreams of me being number one - a leader,
Dad, you knew I could and that was all I needed, thanks.
When the boys banished me from footy,
you battled big,
fathers and their kids,
won the argument.

And I stepped right back upon that pitch.

When I scored halfway against that horrid kid,
you smirked at his dad,
the way you always did.
Because I beat the lads at almost everything.
In time we grew apart with my trauma,
my need for therapists.

That anger burned within me but,
you taught me how to bury it.
How emotion was a detriment, if you let it slip.
I saw you hold your tears, biting at your lips.
You don't show when you're hurt or perishing.
You're a tough man, Dad,
yet, you're scared of everything.

You befriended isolation,
worked, ate, and slept with it.
You never did ask for a hand,
because you're certain no one's genuine.
'If they give, they can take',
lacking trust in everything.
Paranoia always has you questioning.
Now, I do the same, never sure of their intentions – if,
I'm offered any help,
I'm too ashamed to benefit,
and I decline.
I'll be fine.
Why don't you mind your nose?
I'm my daddy's little girl,
I don't need to ask for anything!

If you hide how you feel,
no one can use, abuse or,
mention it.
We laugh pain off, 'act a Jack',
and stay - menacing.
I'm too proud. Too stubborn.
Acts of kindness are so threatening.
The love I know you have,
you're blocked from ever sharing it.
I know, there's many barriers in place.
I'm slowly getting it.
Our situation is too delicate.

We are so similar,
we never quit.
We've made mistakes but learnt to better it.
We're still punishing ourselves for the things we never did.
Always harassed by police in our teens,
our organ disease.
Never rest until we bleed.
We know there are no money trees.
Trying to rectify the many slips and dirty deeds.

Please, don't leave me here. I feel so alone.

It's a shame you rarely call,
we don't hug or connect.
When your girl needs you to walk her through the hell she's in
you're never there.
You know childhood pain morphs into,
adult bitterness.
So, why burn the wood of the bridges,
you haven't finished building yet?

When I bruise, when I cry,
when I'm cold and I'm shivering,
you're my heroine.
You're the one who I'm calling for.
Dismissing hurt as weak,
hidden in the bathroom sobbing, closed down,
I never speak and refuse any comforting.
When they often say;
I'm the image of my father.
I'll assume it's how hardened I have gotten.
How I'm broken, angry, forgotten.
I'm a perfect little picture of my daddy's,
brittle daughter.

I'm a grafter, cause' I'm daddy's little girl.
I learn faster, cause' I'm daddy's little girl.
Confront the hardship, carry daddy, little girl.
Skirt past it for your daddy, little girl.
To much anger, I'm my daddy's little girl.
I am laughed at, just like daddy, little girl.
Deny it's harder cause' I'm daddy's little girl.
It doesn't matter though, I'm daddy's little girl.

Don't they look alike? She's daddy's little girl.
Hide your trauma just like daddy, little girl.
Falling over for her daddy, little girl.
Scraping knees chasing daddy, little girl.
I am frightened, Daddy, hold your little girl.
Stop, Daddy, wait for your little girl.
I am crying, daddy. I'm still a little girl.
Cause' time is dying, dad,
and you won't always have your little girl!

You Will Always Be

I didn't want to hurt you but,
I had to go.
Just know, I'm sorry.
Please, believe - I'm sorry.
Not all souls that roam here can remain in this world.
With every thought of me, inhale every breeze,
cause' while you breathe,
I will always be.

We didn't have the greatest of starts.
The pains of life left in each of us,
the deepest of scars.
Years apart yet, brought together by a purpose,
to change each other's paths,
and we walked many together,
from sunrise until the dark.
Concrete to grass,
spring into Summer,
and as that sun would depart -
you spent long winter evenings cwtched in my arms,
blankets clutched, paws in my palms.
Meaty treats by the fire,
Friends repeats and lengthy trips in the car.
You'd bounce around the living room,
because you knew it made me laugh.

If I ever felt a fear,
your silence brought me some calm.
This emptiness I feel,
it can't be filled, it's so hard.
I look to your space on the sofa,
my voice breaks with my heart.

Your furs still in the carpet,
I pine for your scent and your charm.
My tears are never ending,
walking this journey of ours.

And silence is a reminder,
that you no longer are.

Yet, in those moments between the realms of
wakefulness and sleep,
you approach me, as you always did,
stomping those happy feet.

I cry, with every memory,
yet, that's the love that never truly leaves.
I smile, for always knowing,
I am you, and you,
are me.

You didn't want to hurt me but,
you had to go.
Don't you be sorry.
There is no need to be sorry.
Not all souls that roam here,
can remain in this world.
With every thought you bring,
I inhale every breeze.
While I still breathe,
you - will always be.

The City Part II

These streets recite broken prayers.
from people whose, hope is rare.
Vacant doorways scream stories too sorrowful,
to be spoken there.
Humans lay on concrete, lost in their own despair.
Because we, the people,
treat them like they're ghosts.
Walking, staring through these people like these people aren't our own,
in life we're all taught we should -
fear the unknown.
Fear the unknown.

Tell me, how does this unfold?

Whole families at the food bank,
waiting in the - breadline.
Kids going hungry at - bedtime.
Headlines filled with - tactical blame,
it's a disgusting and in-factual game,
belittling the need for - practical aid.
It's a national shame,
how those on the national wage,
are impoverished.
So wrong - it's
poverty
for all of us but, the elites,
ingrained into our – unsuspecting families.

This is our society.
Causing us insanity.
This is our society.

Killing off our families.
This is our society.
This is **not** society.

They're lying to – each, and every one of us.
They've gotten us to a point we only,
crave for their rottenness.
Throttling us with nine-to-fives,
chained to desks.
They've gotten us – distracted.
Watching clocks.
Comfort sought in substance.
Alcohol.
The lot of us dependent on the hollowest of promises
wallowing in Zombiness,
none of us are happy,
we've forgotten love.
We've forgotten - us.

Graffiti lines the walls,
women walk to catcalls,
hoping not to - flat fall
down streets of
towering - scaffolds.
Anger and abuse whistle, echo
from manholes.
They signal intent yet,
nothing screams fear like a woman
with those keys in her fists,
it's far too treacherous.
Walking alone we are
verbally savaged.
Murdered for our gender,
with a noose on our necks,
our being is ravaged.

But we're your daughters, your mothers, and nanas.
We're your daughters, your mothers, and nanas.
Yet, you burn us if you cannot have us.

Minorities run from authorities on a daily basis.
Policies lack in honesty
and honestly? It's racism.
These people in charge of fake "Great" Britain,
have agendas in motion that remain hidden.
Unforgiving to the skins who fall victim,
inflicted,
by a white-washed prison system.
A white-washed prison system.

Melanin.
Criminal.
Melanin.
Criminal.
Melanin.
Melanin?
Terrorist.

They tell us all be "vigilant".
To keep our wits, be weary of the villainous.
As any time now an 'attack could be imminent'.
Giving no choice but to be deliberate
in prejudice,
step back, people. Here comes an immigrant!
Scrap humanity.
Treat them like they're criminal.
The city has become cynical.
They're clinical to make it difficult.
They want to beat us down,
with subliminal'.

Forcing fear of religion.
We've become so separated,
we no longer identify, with our shared struggles.
That connection is still in us.
Open your eyes, my people.
Just listen
to our talk of division!

Listen, to *their* talk of division.
They manipulate to break our morale and our vision.
Listen, to *their* talk of division.
We are stronger than any credit that they give us.
Listen, to *their* talk of division.
They fear the ignition of that fire deep within us.
Don't listen to *their* talk of division.
They need us at war with each other.
Don't fall for it.
Dismiss it.

Ashes in the Snow

My friends call me; the walking encyclopedia.
My favourite subject at school? History.
I play football... badly.
I love Rice Krispies for breakfast, even at eighteen.
I don't drive yet, but I'm learning.
I have one tattoo (don't tell my mum).
Music... is air.

I have so much to give.
More than my precarious teens would allow to be told.
I am not just a statistic.
A number for you to calculate, and turn into a percentage.
I am not merely a divisive sum to plaster inside the pages of the S@#.
I am somebody's son!

Another's reason to persist and die.

Why is it you forget to acknowledge how I even came to exist,
in your prime-time news at six?
Not one thought of the first kiss,
spawning early morning cups of tea,
and late, late nights.
You erase the laughter and stomach flips,
as bumbling, lusting eyes meet.
The connection of two very different people,
whose love grew me,
placing my pictures on their fridges.
Whose hands would press mine should I fidget.
The begs for books, toys, and stickers,
to which a decline would always result in them,
giving.
The sacrifices of me over them.

Always standing and me, sitting.
Removing their coat to reduce my shivers.
The endless overtime,
twelve-hour shifts in
for happy Christmas dinners.

You've forgotten how these things raised me.
You ignorantly bypass the beginnings.
Entire lives.
The next time you want to hide me in a document,
or file - remember my name.
Which will remain torment for my family.
Who will break themselves fighting for justice,
questioning humanity.
Wondering why me.
That day. That bus stop.
No answers will fill the void their loss, creates.
I missed the bus. And now that impacts all of them.
My parents, friends, teachers, and community.

All of them wounded.
All of them bleed.
All of them die,
along with me.

I don't care for fate.
I refuse to believe my path was made this way.
It was never my time.
Someone stole my future, my life,
all with the grip,
of a knife.
The permanency of a split-second decision.

Siren's approach,
as those who wound scatter and move,
in differing directions.

I glance up from the same concrete I've played kirby,
from underneath the same street lamps that would prompt me home.
Shivering from the cold.
calling for mum, for dad,
yet, lying alone.
My friends called me the walking encyclopedia.
But now?
I'm just ashes in the snow.

All You Ever Say

So, you wake up.
Turn over in bed to gaze outside - you've got to face up.
To another day of play,
you rub your eyes and pick your sane up.
Which shade will you wear today?
Think fake.

The same old faithful?
The same old faithful.

The one that has them convinced "you're cool".
The one that manipulates all of those fools.
Who cross the street cause' grief is contagious,
feet scarper quick as beat,
if you speak your truth.
Brush your teeth and be astute.
Fuck your needs, don't you be so rude!
The bathroom mirror just sneers at you.
Who the hell are you now?
You're even deceiving you.

Don't want to show yourself,
won't reveal who you've come to be.
Every time they ask how you feel,
you close yourself down.
You shrink, playing hide and seek.
All you ever say is;
'I'm alright'.
'I'm fine'.

You grow cold on your own cause'
you don't know,

if they'll cope or fold if you divulge,
so, you show nothing.
Faith flows out of your soul until it dies,
crushing.
Don't hold out for their love,
cause'
the trouble with all your suffering,
is people get weird and they leave if you utter it.
You must sit and cry,
at least try to believe you'll come out of this.
Yes, you want to kill this life,
want to cease but, you're stuck with it.
You can't run away,
there are no retreats,
you better suck it in!

And you shrug again.
Whilst muttering under your breath, that you're struggling.
Refuse to verbalise the blues,
you just smother, cover it.
Look at you, stuttering over your tongue,
it's dumb and you're the dumbest shit.

Who taught you how to hide how you feel?
Insinuated that your feelings are not real?
Who convinced you that crying makes you weak?
Shut you down should you ever speak?
Who forced you into breaking silently?

You don't want to show yourself.
You won't reveal who you've come to be.
Every time they ask how you feel,
you close yourself down,
you shrink, playing hide and seek.
All you ever say is;
'I'm alright'

Aren't you sick of saying,
I'm fine?

'Tiredness kills. Take a break.'

Evrah Introduces Jo Marsh

Jo Marsh works as Creative Director at Ty Pawb, Wrexham and is passionate about art as a tool for social change. Jo is connected to the Association of Arte Util and is part of the related Decentralising Political Economies research project (dpe.tools) with colleagues John Byrne, Alessandra Saviotti and Owen Griffiths. Jo's background is as a freelance artist and arts educator, she also worked as a market trader of Vintage clothing and homewares. In 2011 Jo won the Woolgather Art Prize with her project 'With Love From The Artist', and received grants from Arts Council Wales between 2014 and 2016 to develop and tour her travelling gallery and residency space, Wander Box.

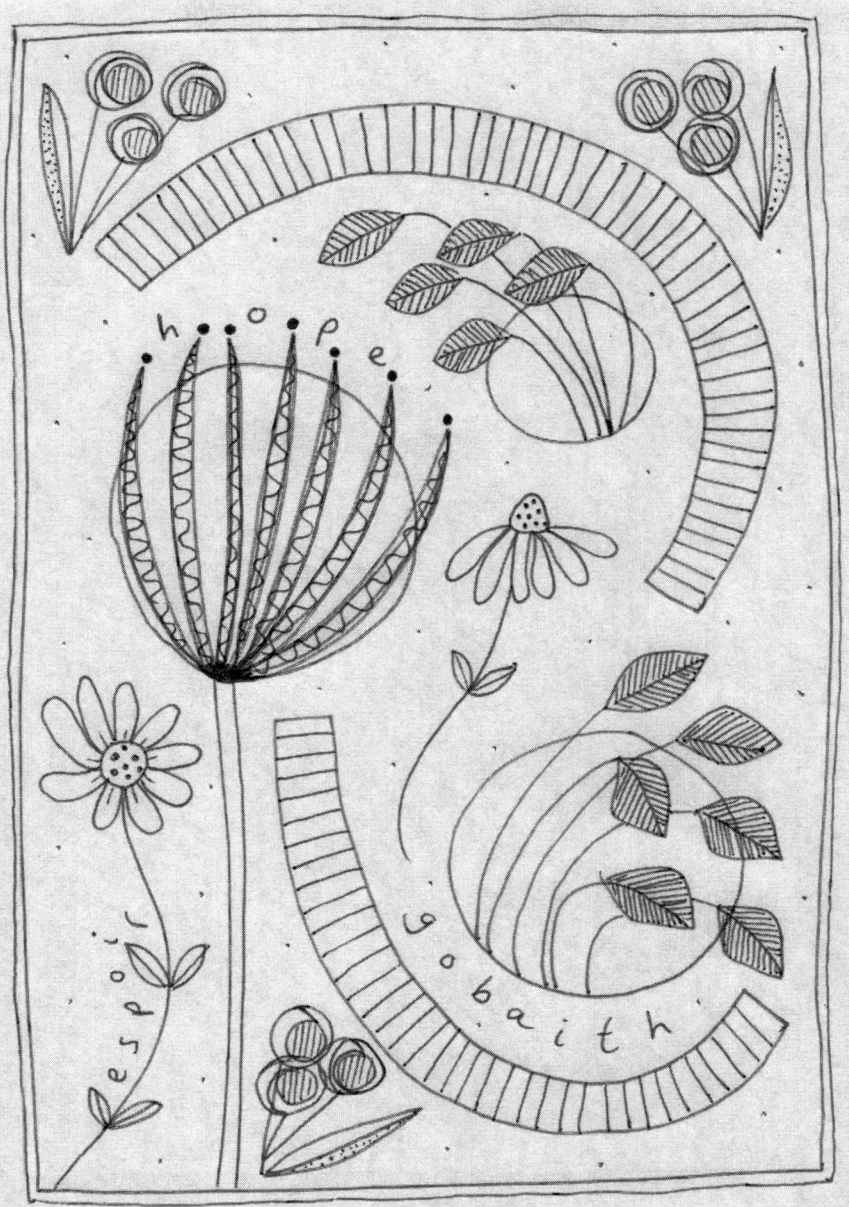

After Nepotism Gains Everyone Loses

We are the choices we make.
We are the lives that could be saved.
When we wake, we can never predict the arrival of an earthquake.
These hard times are hand-picked.
These hard times are herd games.
Sheep dog whistlers rounding us into
one bird cage.

They try to manipulate statistics of how my town is so safe.
Whilst I'm prompted to speak on domestic violence
and crimes borne of hate.
Why don't they take a look at their structures for a minute,
how poorly they support victims?
Not one of them takes time or listens.
And support is delayed until we, give in.

They're always purposely avoiding the real issues.
How anti-racist is now a buzz word used for PR
by those who never fight the cause.
The many barriers intentionally placed before,
people of colour.
Newspapers inciting 'us vs them'.
Black teens handled with brute force,
'wrong place, wrong time',
its aim is to - mute all.

Nothing is changing!

No. I won't focus on my immediate world,
how we're apparently "safe" here and praise it.
When there are many lives right now, fading.

Everyone's homes are caving!

I don't wanna' see another at a food bank.
Hear Universal Credit used to discredit the working-class
because cash flushed muts refuse to give any credit
for the constant obstacles we overcome.
The carefully curated cost-of-living crisis.
Saying goodbye to elderly mums,
who freeze to death in unheated homes.
Leaving behind fathers too vulnerable to live alone.
We fail to care for the people who need it most!
Our children have become our carers,
burdened by the responsibilities we, should be taking on.
Stop romanticising trauma and struggle
as if it's something we excel from.

Social support is crime *prevention*.
Mental health care is suicide *intervention*.
Adequate social housing is life *extending*.
Equity is real *intention*.

You talk change as if it's something you want to engage.
As if it's something you believe in.
Nothing materialises from your meetings.
No movement, motivation or feeling.
You want to know how you elicit positive change?
You change thoughts, governments, and laws.
Stop criminalising people.
End this so-called "drug war".
Stop labelling asylum seekers as illegal.

Geography defines our worth.
Children should be playing freely, digging in dirt.
Instead, they're digging their own graves,
with a deep hunger and thirst.
Because, poverty here, is hereditary now.

A hand me down apathy.

You may dislike these words.
The way I choose to pen verse
yet, this uncomfortable truth is the harsh reality,
for families standing next to a hearse.
Loved one's names sculpted from flowers,
that'll live longer than any of the feeble,
empty promises,
you will never care to serve.
Too many spend their lives bleeding for a system,
with poor working conditions and inadequate pay.
You push blame onto those who've no options, no headspace.
Policing our voices,
freedoms are fair game.
Now, we have no room for mistakes.
Our rights are being steadily erased.

I can't do this anymore!

I can't keep sweeping your floors,
creating fake positivity to paint upon these crumbling walls.
It's nothing but a stall to buy time we cannot afford.
The dwindling healthcare you've built careers and cash to destroy.

You ask me to speak to the people.
But, which one of *you* speaks for the people?

The cheek of you saying our youth have gone astray,
when they're trapped within an environment
that restricts their ability to express or play.
I'm so tired of being used to say something.
I'm so tired of being moved to change, nothing!

Don't talk to me about your hopes.
Don't stand there lying through your crooked teeth.

You only intend to support the "elite".
When our communities ask you to meet their needs
you slam every single door.
We deserve more!

People cannot grow or hold onto belief,
when you stifle every opportunity they seek.
This isn't working!
We cannot have another cry for a lost love.
We cannot have another family hurting.

Because, we are every choice you make.
And we, are the lives that must be saved.
When you walk away, from another fake political rally,
with written speeches stolen from historical templates,
remember
you have the power to break this cycle of pain.
Do not allow another to slip away.

'Big deal, I whistled at you like a dog. So, fucking what. Get over it'

Run Away

Too many people to often say;
'When you end your struggle, you're just forwarding that pain'.
Onto those still left. Those who remain.
That's something that those without an inclination say.
Deflecting the feelings of being impaled.
Stuck in a terrible situation that - you did not create.
An appearance that - you cannot maintain.
Every morning, disappointed that you wake.
Counting down the hours
until you can go back to bed again.

I hear 'it's okay not to be okay'.
Just try mention suicide, people freak and turn away.
Load you with guilt trips to convince you to stay.
They can't find it in themselves to normalise the openness,
and attempt to conversate.
You're uncomfortable, as a result,
I feel ashamed.
Still, you wonder why people don't talk,
withdraw, and eventually isolate?
I don't have the energy to dress and fake a smile today.
Yet, I have to engage, and act a part in your play,
to make you feel safe.

Where are you when I don't feel safe?
Where are you when I stumble in the kitchen doorway?

Where are you when I stare at the rain through a window of a house
I can rarely escape?
When my speech fails and I cannot express or stipulate, how I feel,
or the times when I'm betrayed by the food on my plate?
Choking on my spaghetti.

You claimed you'd never forget me.
Yet, the only time I receive a text is when you need my name
to generate
something for your cause.
Rarely ask if I'm okay,
no support.
When I cancel plans you always seem to sigh and frustrate,
not understanding that simple tasks can quite often take,
quadruple the time.

Just look at my face, do I really look happy?
Why won't you just grant me
the freedom to break?
When was the last time you called, visited, or checked in?
Why can't I cry without your obligates?

Instead, I'm lost in this space,
full of sadness and anxiety.
Where the hell is my family?
Where's the concern?
Where are the asks after me?
They're scamming me.
I gave up so much of my time, so many parts of me.
Now they're AWOL and excuse it,
by accusing me of being distant.

Have you tried giving your soul when your soul has gone missing?
When you're dealing with a chronic condition?
When brushing your teeth is energy killing,
and the pain you endure is so, fucking unforgiving?
And the language that served as a friend,
continues to diminish.
When everything you'd built for yourself fades
with your identity and vision?
When your future and ambition hang on a thread.
You part with your problems,

if I try to talk about mine, you're always dismissive.

I didn't ask for this life,
the shitty cards I've been given.
I swear if my legs would carry me,
I'd be gone in an instant.
I'm here wishing,
one day I'll get eternal rest
from the hell that is living.

Let Them Eat Cake

Turn off the news again.
It's just a fuel to them. No truth from men,
trying to cover up their deviance.
Another winner? A gloveless crude defence.
Striking strikers, blues and twos as well.
Moved by their defiance,
I'm reminded of all the times I said I'd move but spent,
days stuck here in my bed, without objective.

I Idly choose to fence,
myself within this brazen cage.
Disillusioned, bemusing friends.
They misunderstand why I refuse to glue myself,
to ideas pushed by pointless peer pressure,
and carefree movie men.
With their cash and clothes,
flashy jewels, the Benz - yet,
all of them glitters never brought me anything other
than useless users – guess,
I'm confined to this appertaining rage of injustice. A
s a pacifist and socialist, devoid of purpose,
passion potent yet,
unable to harness, motivate or govern it.

The government has plenty ways of killing us,
emotionless.
Coping strategies lost to the cowardice of clowns and jokers – kiss,
a friend on the lips and you're risking catching COVID -
kids unsocialised, poking holes in those without a decent phone
or Prime on socials - sick.
Sleep deprived in steep anxiety, exams, coerced, indoctrinated.
Stiff governance of thought, designed to leave them broken,

motionless.

Why don't you give a moment then,
to all those trapped within the throws of loneliness?
Our isolated elderly searching for someone to provide them comforting,
a little something – where,
are your congruencies?
Inconsistencies in every sentence written, spoken - shared.
We spread their lies.
We're their pigeon postal pets.
The ones pumping all that hot and pungent air,
into aggressive, ill-intentioned, and repressive bills.

Parting with our social cares.

Laws attract only those who can afford to pay them - thrilled,
by the harbours of Monaco, off the shore the waters still.
Skate on ice, there's no easy way, but we have our Wills.
Still, confronting bare reality, it rarely comes with ease.
When the sleazy media manipulates, manages, and extorts the truth.

The truth.
The truth?
What is the truth?
Can you tell me? Cause' fuck.
I can't be telling you!

We're so deep in this now,
we've no way of knowing who we are or how to choose – shit,
what is it then that I'm supposed to do?
Get up off this sticky sofa?
Snap out of this chronic mood?
Motivate and inspire myself?
Turn the tele on and gorge on the latest colonic news?
Nah, I'd rather be alone sat here ruminating on my mistakes

within these blues.

At least it's real, somewhat logical.
Something I've become accustomed to.
A customed custom conjured up,
a packaged bolstered grudge,
to feed off freely.
I cuss and bust a gut,
while allowing all these cluster fucks to cut another cut,
from which another must suffer – look,
it's just a dusting on
the sponge of a multi-layered cake we slice,
and loath yet, all consume.

Lol. Why are you crying?

What's your problem? You have issues.
You're far too - sensitive.
Maybe it's, I don't know... Because you're a feminist?
You're just too deep, you can never take a joke!
Oh, God! Why are you always so - offended?
Woof, woof. Your foods' done – come and get it!
So, what? I said that you looked pregnant.
No, I wouldn't say that to my mum or friends. They don't.
When I said it to you, it's because I meant it.
You're twisting up the context.
That's not how I worded anything, or remember it.
I am being unfairly misrepresented!
Get a grip!

Have you not taken your meds again? You'll cheat on me without them.
You need those heavy pills I force down your throat.
Watching carefully as you swallow.
You seem awfully enthused with the news and politics.
Are you ok? Are you psychotic?
Are you sure you're really experiencing what you think you are?

Here's a present.
I didn't obtain your dead Granddad's jacket to look attentive.
Not to manipulate the situation enough to make you question reality.
To forget all the truths I'm busy bending.
the excuses, abuses, and mangling of every sentence.
To rattle your intuition
endless,
are my ill intentions to make you stay.
I will tell them 'you're mental'
if you dare mention my wrongs again.

Mrs. perfect. You act like you're some fucking angel.
You're pathetic.
So ungrateful and overly expectant.
Such a drain.
Forever difficult to manage and maintain.
There's no easy way to restrain you -
so, it's time to up the pressure.
These remaining relationships of yours,
I must fragment them.
Quite frankly, you're offensive.
I do support you, look at all I've done.
You idiot, you're too emotional. Always moaning so – dramatic!
Lol, why are you crying? You need to calm down.
Take a chill. You're manic.

No, don't leave the house, you're too vulnerable.
COVID will kill.
How will you leave? You've no money.
Your parents don't care, don't go.
It makes no sense to leave.
Home is miles away. Don't book the train,
you're too weak.
You have it good with me.
Such a victim, aren't you? Always accusatory.
Ha you're struggling to breathe. Baby, take a seat.
Do you want something to eat? Pasta with cheese?
Wait, where are you going?
It's too cold out there, you'll freeze!
Take my coat. What about your poor knees?
You'll be in too much pain, hun.
If you need help, will you phone me?

Money? No, you don't need your savings.
They're for our future. For me.
You have everything that you could need,
right here is where you should be.

I don't understand why you say all of these nasty things,
when I'm the only one who is ever there for you.
I swear I will change. Why do you not believe?
It's just a blip, a slip,
a mistake of youth, you see?
I'm no wife beater. Don't exaggerate it, please.
I was merely pushing you, there was no malice behind my feet.
No intent with the double kick that came from my bent knees.
It wasn't a thrust ensuring you wouldn't out my numerous,
disgusting deeds.
It wasn't a blunt force to damage you.
Anyway, it's your fault.
You cause my issues with anger management.

The fractured ribs are just an accident.
Let me heal your wounds, laugh, build up your hopes,
and then, dismantle them.
I'll promise you the world whilst working to tarnish it.
I'm sorry you feel this way.
I'm so stressed and struggle to handle it.
You're my everything, and all I adore.
Don't add to my inner sadness.
My double standards.
The tourniquet I wrap around it.
Don't be silly, this was all just a gross misunderstanding – bitch,

I hate you. I love you.
You're killing our lovely marriage.
I will manipulate everyone, convince them of your madness,
park outside the house and creep around rattling,
the bins and recycling, frighten you and the dogs,
until fear has you scrambling,
to barricade the doors and windows,
call you constantly. Maintain the harassment.
You can't block me or leave - I will find you.

I will pack up and start travelling
the three hours to your parents to give you syringes.
Your birthday will be tarnished with anxiety,
nausea, and sickness.
I control the narrative. I'm the winner in this.
Why are you so stubborn and unforgiving?
I did nothing wrong, you're overacting, I wish you'd give in!

I need to be holding your hand in old age,
why take our dream and ravage it?
Ignore the times I held you down,
the times I gripped you, strangling.
Kept you confused, uncertain - dangling.
On the threads of nothingness.
Backhanders, sick jokes,
and the years of emotional damages.
You're amazing. You slut.
Living life without you
just isn't worth imagining.

'If your purpose in any conflict is to win. Whether that be in intimate relationships, family or other. You're not seeking change, equity or understanding. You're wanting power.'

My Sister's Keeper

I couldn't let you cut your feet,
so, I held on to your hands too tightly,
resulting in injury.
The shame I feel extends beyond the years we've had to bleed.
I know you feel no anger or hate towards me.
But, that lesson early on taught me things you never read.
Never hear and never see.
If anything, it's become a defining entity.

Nothing articulates this inner need,
to be a silent protector, emotionally and physically,
watching over you in waking life and in your dreams.
Distracting you with jokes and games when you couldn't sleep.
Keeping guard as you played within the street.
Listened intently when you developed a sudden wheeze.
Pushed you to believe in yourself, that you could achieve.
When they caused you to cry,
I beat your bullies thoroughly.
I pounded every nasty from their lips,
until they couldn't breathe.
It's simple, really.
They go at you, you come for me.

When school divided us,
It's something I could not accept,
I'd spend every lunchtime at the gate,
watching, waiting for my friend.
As kids poured onto the yard,
I'd search for your smiling face cause',
there is nothing in this world that could degrade our bond,
or separate us.

Growing had us walking different paths from the ones we shared as kids.
You knew my need to move beyond the world in which we lived.
I had to find my own way and you understood why I left the way I did.
I needed time and independence,
space to escape - everything.
When Fix You hit the radio, we'd often cry.
We'd voice note the chorus and curse on every mile.
Yet, distance never could diminish or sever ties.
We're Nammy – my twin.
They couldn't break us if they tried.

I don't know how life will change or where we're gonna' go.
I can't predict the future or give you answers to all you wanna' know.
I can't promise my years won't be shorter than we'd wanna hope.
There are many things uncertain, my care is not one of those.

When I say I have your back, always know this truth – this love.
The world may break its promises, that's something
I never would.
If doubt cripples your confidence, I am a voice that you can trust.
I will guide you through every pain you're never treading dust.

On the day I left for Newport
I remember the heavy looks.
Trying to hide the emotions we knew would bury us.
As I walked away from your car,
I glanced back to where you stood.
I said I'd come back for you sister, just as soon as I could.
My word is good.
Cause'

If I should ever have to leave ya.
I'll forever be your keeper.
When the world feels heavy, when you're fearful.
Just call my name, little sister,
I will hear ya.

If I should ever have to leave ya.
I'll forever be your keeper.
When the wounds hurt plenty, when you're tearful.
You call my name, little sister,
I will heal ya.

*Pump them fists to your chest,
use any crutch you can find.
With every strength that you have,
lift up your head with that pride,
you've always had deep inside.
Don't you collapse and then die,
Don't you dare fold and retire,
get off that floor and you try!*

Sign Anguish

Living feels very much a cycle, doesn't it? An arduous canyon of pain.
Trying, man, the trying – always feels in vain.
One struggle, to the next.
Your efforts, a waste.
The many substances to anaesthetise,
and you're sick of the taste.
Still, you stick to the same,
unable to switch up this state.

Just know, somewhere, someone is thinking of you.
As they go about their day, a smile breaks a commonly fixed frown,
with a momentary, welcomed distraction.
You change their life by simply, existing,
being the person, you feel is lost.
Hear what I'm saying?
When you really think about it,
isn't that something?
It's magic, don't you agree?
A spark. A calling to stay, maybe?

Despite the lies your worried,
exhausted mind would have you believe.
And the endless, mounting trials
from which your energy depletes and
never heals.
You're a glow to another, feeling much like you do.
Reflective and in need of a sign too.

As your fingers curl,
and regret wraps itself around your thoughts,
extending to those you love but feel you burden.
Listen,

for this is a little understood yet, real fact.
One we all should know.
We all should hone.

Our existence is our purpose.

It's an untold reminder.
A motive another finds strength in to go on.
And you, must go on too.
Wipe your tears, take a breath,
and reflect on the light you've found in others.
It's the same light they find - in you.
Notice how your presence brings a needed whisper,
for another to hold on?
Don't fall for the manipulative darkness.
Kick your heels defiantly at that muted fade and deny the dusk.
Although the sun's gone,
I promise, it won't always be.
You have to run on.
Please, run on.
We need you.
You're a reason,
a hero
to someone.

Twelve Thirty-Three

With the dying of the daylight,
soft glows peaked over the peaks.
We'd wake, break in the doorways,
whilst the sun began its sleep.
Shit talking. Planning trips.
Fantasies of who we might be,
without caution for anything,
full house at number twenty, sweet!

I fiddle with old ideas,
and the roughed edges of my sleeves.
Trying to break this tension somehow,
but it seems it won't relieve.
I'm always compelled to fidget,
stop, and then repeat,
in any tough situation,
which annoyed you endlessly.

The bass shakes up the windshield.
Speakers vibrate vibrantly.
I'm lost within the dubs, loud vox yet,
I'm hurting silently.
I open up the glove box,
roll and spark another, jeez.
How many more can I smoke this evening avoiding how I feel?

Can't dim the voice inside,
I try to convince myself it's weak.
That there's no strength within its words
when it intrudes to say to me;
you're just another lost one,
like all of them other teens.

I turn the volume up to forty,
and pick at the stain left in my jeans.

Unsettled by uncertainty,
I'm unsure if I'll ever get to see,
a day where you genuinely laugh again,
as your eyes well up and crease.
Dancing with the happiness, you did way back with me.
Where Adagio for Strings rung out,
blanks were filled in by your keys.

Sad and harder times, they say they come in threes.
Regrets they always cry the loudest,
and they pitch to low, cut deep.
Didn't spend enough though, did we?
Should have slowed down those memories.
We spent them all too recklessly.
Naive fools waste time dining cheap.

You were skipping in your trainers,
snow fights and late brekkies at F&B's.
LED's, car bonnet bangers,
but, next thing, the rhythm changed within a blink.

Beyond this car interior, can you hear our melody?
I'll play another tune for you, as I bounce here in my seat.
If you're ever coming back, trust that there will be,
a playlist waiting for you, no doubt.
A build, drop, ciggy and a drink.
twelve thirty three.
Call Me

Imprints

No one is timeless.
However, please be mindful of the ripples you generate in life, as they just might be.
Leave something behind that empowers and inspires.
That instigates an enduring flame.
When our physical existence on this earth ceases,
it isn't the words and thoughts of our loved ones that will define us only.
It will be the motion and embers left glowing within strangers and those who've no
reason to speak of us via thoughtfully expressed love notes or, eulogies.
And so, the question remains.
How do you want to be remembered?
What type of footprint are you creating?
Before you depart,
leave a legacy and never a scar.

Call Me Home

It's that time of year again.
Where we gather with our family, lovers,
and our friends.
Packed living rooms, crippled by
overindulgence,
Mindlessly stressing over cutlery, guests,
and chairs.
I try my best but, it's impossible to pretend
I'm invested.

That heavy, pressing ache within my
throat from swallowed tears,
forces me outside to take some time,
inhale as I reflect on passing years.
Everyone looks real happy,
so full of cheer.
I can't join in joking, laughing knowing

you're not here.

I haven't been able to visit you.
I haven't been able to sit with this truth.
I'm healing slowly still, this emptiness is
bitter – you,
always told me I should take my time,
slow down within my youth.
I didn't listen, I rushed around,
I didn't give all I could have given you.

It's difficult,
dealing with this hidden guilt.
I'm unable to move on because I feel like

I'd be giving up.
on your life,
your love,
your memory,
I'm too afraid to break this rut but,
I'm not living, just
existing
wandering empty rooms for
your touch.

I'm so terrified of closure though.
And deep down I guess I've always known.
You'd never want this grief for me,
a burning anger that seems to hold
my words, my ability to call her phone.

It's time for me to let you go.
If I don't, I know I will never grow.
I promise you'll forever be a part of me,
my anchor, my grounding
in every storm,
until the day you raise your arms in embrace
and call me home.

I feel them aiming at me.
Taking shots with the hope that I'd bleed.
Look how hate becomes the mind.
But no matter how deep
your wounds, I will rise from these knees.
And they'll forget your name in time.
That's how you'll live and die.

'And that's it, isn't it? She isn't being spoken about. Not in the way she believes she's entitled to or, how we speak of those who bring light to us.

Eventually, no one will think of her at all. She'll be forgotten.

No one will sit and reflect warmly on how she supported and pulled them through, nor how she changed their life in any meaningful way. They will never wonder where or, how she is. From that alone, a conversation will never materialise with another. Not one loving expression. Like all things without positive purpose, there will be silence where once there was pain'.

Role Models

We watch the trodden die.
Silent is the suffering from those who live a 'common life'.
I observe another lie.
Can't find a minute of release from all the shit that I'm so bothered by.
They won't apologise.
Denial in a Kingdom reduced to hatred,
produced to traumatise,
anyone who may speak up.

These are hard lines.

And I link up with a friend,
stressing over living costs, the figures, and the trends.
They're getting richer, suits are slicker whilst we all just try to make an ends.
Scrimping, scraping but, we've nawt left,
our cupboards bare.
It's our fault, it's our flaws, it's our pain to share.

Isn't it?

We're the ones creating the struggles we are living with.
We're the ones hiking inflation and killing businesses.
Sinking the NHS whilst giving offshores to our "business friends".
We're increasing taxes, wiping emails, dodging scrutiny.
Financing dodgy PPE.

They're the fact-less, scandalous, and backless.
Predators with crack ships,
they delegate their seedy greed.
Now the public have no room to argue or to breathe.
We are stuck here now it seems.

Don't you say a word, pleb.
The police will have you cuffed and seized.
You can be convicted now if you protest in the streets.

You better cease.

How can they close another eye?
Watch a family break,
hardship a hard shift to be swallowed by,
the poverty handed down by those living their corporate lives,
claiming they're "elite",
what's elite about those other guys?
Speeding past the working-class in their motors - mime,
obscenities.
The scene it stinks of coke and lies.

What's classy if you're rich but, scummy if you're poor?
Crooked sticks draw straight lines behind the toilet doors.

Hands up skirts, gropes in a darkened cornered world.
You'll be black balled heavy if you speak,
don't you spoil it girl.
Your career will be dead by the morning, girl.
So, here's your warning, girls.

Get a book deal, don't write a page,
and extort the public purse.
Lie to royalty, chill in an empty fridge,
indulge in shopping sprees at Selfridges.
No exerting selflessness.
Cheat on your spouse,
publicly fund your house,
and deny your many kids.
Etonian dystopias, malicious sentiments,

the common life.

Drunks in the chambers, picking fights,
last order of the night,
the sworded types,
born of white,
staggering,
mindless heckles, mixers and some gambling.

Don't you be breaking mirrors in the cabinet.

Quarrelling, office skits,
Sky news ramblings,
when you're off your tits.
False promises of funding for the hospitals,
and the hospices.
Cutting services, and libraries,
followed with fake tears for the losses which
your many pals are profiting.

Party whilst the nation buries coffins – if,
you're asking for my role models – it's,
the Trusses and the Moggs,
the Thatcher's and the Boris's.
I'm inspired just watching them,
to be their very opposite.
Up the Workers, comrades,
they're my people,
and I pay them homages.

Cycles

She would cry, as soon as he would leave a room.
Told he would be back, she would chase, at the heels of his shoes.
A trip to the shops, to grab some bread and milk,
always filled her with anxiety, this girl had seen the blood get spilled.
She applied that experience to every trip,
if he can hurt in his home, surely out the door he would be hit?
She was just a kid, how was she to understand any part of this?
To watch a grown man cry and cower into something small,
even though - he was big.
Lacking structure, safety, like every kid, she needed it.
Burdened with the parent role,
adult punches thrown and she stood refereeing it.
'Watch your feet, little sis, that glass is dangerous,
here, let me clean this bit'.

Glasses, lagers hurled in front of a girl,
who'd carry that same anger from the living room,
into the wider world.
Became the very hate that raised her,
as she raged at society's failures.
And with all those lessons' life had gave her,
She'd use her fists first and ask them questions later.

Pain was all that seemed to last.
For her, it's continuity was a definite comfort,
I know, it's sad - but,
at least she could rely on that,
the only hug that held her,
searching for love, hard souled and vulnerable
to all who would befriend her.
Began stealing for friends,
for fear they'd resent and unfriend her.

Easily manipulated by poison elders.
The Police knew her well,
a free falling and delinquent drunken youth.
Mental health? Declining too.
School couldn't (wouldn't) support her, what did they decide to do?

Banish her from education.
They lacked the care and dedication,
to see past her issues,
she was simply more statistics for their papers.
A teen without a future,
so much potential to result in failure.
She knew their game,
she knew the label they stamped and gave her.
She stood tall and refused to take it.
Made a personal promise to enact some changes.
Took those losses, internal rages,
her experiences,
and the many difficult phases,
and let her pen bleed her pain,
on to every one of her journal pages.

She clawed her way right out of those cracks,
with an empathy and understanding,
no one ever cared to pay her.
Became her own role model,
with a mindful self-reflection,
and often tempered patience.
She wobbled and laboured.
Hurt with every story told yet, she never gave up.
Worked hard on herself,
forgave her mistakes,
grafted though it was painful.
Yes, she made it.
Don't forget these kids are your neighbours.
What saved her?

Breaking the vicious cycle
that had always choked and chained her.

We can all take our future and change it.
Yes, it hurts, the past will always be painful.
Our children need love, be courageous.
It's on us to break the hatred that raised us.

All I Need Is Time

I pulled on my last fraying thread, completely undoing myself.
Unravelling all the bits you had woven in - to me,
until I was,
cotton spaghetti.
Hours upon hours I spent in that mayhem,
lying amongst my many pieces,
dwelling on the form I - once was.
Grieving, for the myth you, had me believe.
Only the walls know just how I cried for the parts of me,
I thought were lost.
And the moments, I had no ability to change.
Chronically fatigued from, holding on.

You want to know the strange thing about letting go?
The thought of doing so,
is much harder than the action itself.
Embrace the feeling of fear.
Acknowledge the tension it brings because,
once you open those palms,
drop the shoulders and your lungs - exhale,
you truly, become.

No more slumber.

As I awoke, I reached for the sharpest needle I could find.
Picked up what I could salvage and began recreating something,
from those disordered remains.
Each new stitch was slow, and painful work.
Not every one was right or, perfect – yet,
with that labour,
the chaos became something, meaningful,
something, whole again.

Only this time, it wasn't made by you.
It was my creation.
With the conscious choices, I made.
The light, shade, and quirks I wanted,
which I affectionately named;
My Best Self.
And, you know what?

I fucking love her.

Wander Gently as You Go

The world has us convinced that certain metrics and benchmarks
define our lives.
I should do this by twenty-five. I should be married with children at thirty. I should bemore together by now. I haven't achieved this or that.
Look, everything has its own time.
Stop comparing yourself to others.

It's the same with our hearts and minds. We place priority on how
others believe we should feel,
and waste too much time keeping up appearances, masking.
We need to allow ourselves to grieve, to feel anger and sadness. To live
and experience those emotions.
Because, emotions are extreme but, they're supposed to be.
It's a cruel injustice we inflict upon us when we force ourselves,
not to feel something.
The dynamics of those differing shades.

Happiness isn't a constant.
It's unnatural to feel happy one hundred percent of the time.
With much pain, comes much gratitude.
We're so focused on this constant need to please, to smile we wind up missing the parts of life that add those little flickers of contentment
we're searching for.
They simply, pass us by.
Feel the grass beneath your bare feet. Take in and embrace the breeze.
Close your eyes, look up and feel the warmth of the sun on your face,

stop for a second.
Feel what it is you're feeling.
Just – let it in.

We're quick to push things that need to be given space to
breathe and materialise.
Everyone has an opinion on what you should and shouldn't do.
We often make decisions for ourselves that, aren't right.
Based on what others believe.
We need to give ourselves kindness, allow freedom to become,
who – we want to be.
It isn't an easy process and no, it won't happen overnight. That's okay.
There's no definitive in anything – there are no certainties.
Sometimes, you'll be ahead. Other times – you'll fall.

Yet, that's how we learn,
that's how we change.

If it means something to you, take your time.
Wander gently as you go.
It's your life, do it at your own pace, in your own way, you know?
Be kind. Give space. Nurture your body, your mind, and goals.
Let that love – be slow.
After all, you can't rush growth.

For Every Step

When I wake of a morning, too fatigued to be contemplative.
And these bones of mine scream for rest, for patience.
When my palpitating heart jumps between resistance and aching,
and I am too heavy to hold my own weight.
I'm reminded daily that every pavement I'm pacing,
is laced by the people I draw faith from,
have faith in.

I cry, I cry so fucking much,
debates of vacating this brutal landscape,
I'm forever wading.
And in those darkest, most disgustingly rage-filled, breakings.
When to be alone is easier than faking.
And to fall, is easier than taking another day in.
I'm driven to be the catalyst,
with or without the lights or stages.
Because, I know,
just one more day upon this earth
could be the day we change things.
Just one more minute,
could create the cascading rain to renew.
Whether this body can move any further,
than the small steps I tire making,
is something I cannot bet upon, find security or, safety.
Yet, our freedom is worth the struggle in chasing.
My strength is guided by the words and exchanges,
with those who walk beside this,
tenacious, can't quite find the words wordsmithing,
sometimes weak, sometimes courageous,
forever regenerating, impatient patient.
It is you that saves this body so wasted.
You, and your many crying,

beautiful,
hopeful faces.

I am truly grateful for every step you carry me.
Diolch o galon,
caru ti.

I left you once

I hear the way that they talk about you.
How they, label, distrust and degrade all our youth.
How they, take their hits on the pages, the news.
The snide comments, there's no escaping those fools.
As I walk through your alleys,
I hold a deep understanding,
of how buried you are within my goals.
And they will just never know how I feel,
when I see your – signs.
Every day and night, I want to scream,
it's – why.
Wherever I go - believe me, I chime.
Caia for the win. Up the Park!
The Sunnyside.

No matter how we grow I've realised,
that when we rise, they try to deny it.
Work hard to deprive us,
then ride us.
But they don't know how deep this pride goes,
La, we're survivors!
With all the shots they throw,
they couldn't fight us.
So, when I look up at that sky
I know,
I am blessed because my hometown,
gave me this soul,
and I glow.

Cause' we are rich in history.
They struggle to understand how this grit is innate.
It seems such a mystery.

To all those who've never walked these streets,
okay, come visit me.
I'll show you how we turn our darkness
into the brightest of imagery.
The ingenuity that's present in us all
impressive, you would say?
Many thought that we'd never succeed,
we'd bend and break,
I guess it's special, in a way.
How around the globe they know us.
How they overlooked us
yet, we progress these many lanes,
you better sing and praise

Wrecsam is the name.

Look how the mighty raise.
How we grapple with the greats.
You better stand and ovate,
clap your hands and don't hate,
how we grew from our pain.

Wrecsam is the name.

This is for my hometown.
Sending love to my hometown.
I left you once but, I'm home now.

I'm home now.

DEFINEHOPE

WE EACH SPEND OUR LIVES SEARCHING,
NEEDING SOMETHING TO GRASP IN TIMES OF UNCERTAINTY.
A SIGN, PROMPT, A PRESENCE OR DEFINITION.
SOME REACH FOR RELIGION. OTHERS, MUSIC.
WE DO AND CLUTCH WHAT WE CAN TO PULL US THROUGH
THE PAIN OF OUR WAVERING FAITH,
DURING THOSE
MOMENTS OF SOLITARY FEAR.
YET, THERE IS THIS ONE PHENOMENON WE ALL SHARE.

IT'S IN THE HANDS WE HOLD, OUR WORDS OF COMFORT
AND EMBRACE.
THE LIGHT WE PROVIDE AND POSSESS.
JUST AS EVERY RIVER FLOWS FROM DENSE WOODLAND TO
OPEN SEAS,
THE WORLD. OUR WORLD, IN ALL ITS VASTNESS
IS DEEPLY CONNECTED.
WE, AS HUMAN BEINGS, REGARDLESS OF OUR FOOTSTEPS
- HEAVY OR LIGHT –
ARE UNITED BY HOPE.
AND, JUST LIKE WATER,

IT RUNS THROUGH EACH AND EVERY ONE OF US.

ACKNOWLEDGEMENTS

Spoz - thank you for bringing us home. My gratitude extends far beyond anything I could possibly write.

Sammy - my twin, my people. You came at me with the words I needed to hear. The very words that moved me to fight. What you did for me in my darkest moments can't be overstated. Thanks, man!

Yazzy - thank you for the long chats and card readings. For giving me an avenue to open up when I needed it most. For having my back and believing in my painful truth. I will never forget.

Lillie - the most brilliant mind of anyone I know. You kept me going at my most lonely; that much needed spark. Know you are gifted beyond measure and I truly believe you'll change this world in some way. You're gonna go far, kid.

To the silent hero. For the many trips, wheelchair crashes, appointments, late late nights and early mornings. The numerous ucomfortable hospital chairs and sleep deprivation and stair lifts. For laughing along with me with every bit of bad news and speaking when I was voiceless. For the many phone calls, scans and tests. The frustrations, mediations, tears and breakthroughs. The journey is far from over but, the worst I feel, just might be. Thank you!

Hendricks and Paisley - my protectors. Without you, I simply wouldn't have survived.

To my town - the greatest community of people on earth. I came back to you broken, exhausted and in need of comfort and purpose. You provided - in the most brilliant Wrecsam way. I am who I am, because of you.

Up the Town!

Live Fear Free
0808 80 10 800

ABOUT VERVE POETRY PRESS

Verve Poetry Press is an award-winning press that focused initially on meeting a local need in Birmingham - a need for the vibrant poetry scene here in Brum to find a way to present itself to the poetry world via publication. Co-founded by Stuart Bartholomew and Amerah Saleh, it now publishes poets from all corners of the UK - poets that speak to the city's varied and energetic qualities and will contribute to its many poetic stories.

Added to this is a colourful pamphlet series, many featuring poets who have performed at our sister festival - and a poetry show series which captures the magic of longer poetry performance pieces by festival alumni such as Polarbear, Matt Abbott and Imogen Stirling.

The press has been voted Most Innovative Publisher at the Saboteur Awards, and has won the Publisher's Award for Poetry Pamphlets at the Michael Marks Awards.

Like the festival, we strive to think about poetry in inclusive ways and embrace the multiplicity of approaches towards this glorious art.

www.vervepoetrypress.com
@VervePoetryPres
mail@vervepoetrypress.com